A moment's knowing

Lyndsey Rule

BookLeaf
Publishing

India | USA | UK

Presentation by *BookLeaf Publishing*

Web: www.bookleafpub.com

E-mail: info@bookleafpub.com

ISBN: 9789358738438

First edition 2023

For my Mum.

Colours of a January day

My soul is as
Colourful as this
Old January day -
Grey.

My soughing, blustery thoughts
Are not grey; they are anything but
They are
Black and blue
And red and yellow and
Orange and purple and
Brown

...and...

You know how,
If you blend together
All the colours of the rainbow,

You get brown?
(Or with colours made of light,
White?)

Well. If you
Blend together all the

Colours of my brain,
You get:

Grey.
The watery, blurry monochrome
Of a dull, January day.

Of short daylight hours.
Of cold rain spitting
On a sharp leafless hedge.

Of a slow-sliming snail.
Of mud, and puddles,
Boots and anoraks

(What a grey word
Is 'anorak'!)

Of robin-song hung out to dry
On the still, damp, still-damp, nothing air

Of Nothing, there.

I am not dull though.
Despite the grey;
Not really.

It is a necessary,
Sleepy, hibernation-cosy

Soft sort of grey.

The sort of grey that
- one day -
- eventually -
Suddenly seems
To have precipitated out into

Green.

Easter 2017

We made
it through that time of hardship,
cold and scarcity:
winter

weathered
by another year; reborn,
life is springing forth
again

in green;
rushing to relate the tale,
"we survived! We're
alive!"

Ewe 212

She walks over to me and
Sniffs my hair,
Warm, woolly breath tickling
As I sit, leaning

Against the smooth, wooden beams
Of the hurdle edge of
The straw-strewn fold.

This time last year,
Within the safety of
These self-same hurdle walls
She was born,

A tint, soaking, black, woolly scrap of life
Fighting
To swap air for mucus
To stand on misbehaving, wobbly, too-long legs
To search out that all-important source
of strength-giving food-warmth

The ewe - fretting -
Calls to her child
Licks and nibbles at the clinging birth fluids and
Circles - forgetting

To stand,
Torn between the need for her to drink
And the need to know her.

Her butting bullet head closes in
After her minutes-old naïveté finally dismisses
Mucky hanging wool dogs,
Instincts, willpower -
and a shepherds guiding kindly hands -
find the tear; she grasps and suckles strongly
Her first crucial taste:
"75 'elephants'...
...she'll do."

The Wood

I walked into the wood
At dusk
And stood.

Crying out, the birds
Gossiped,
Wondering.

The trees turned and
Looked at me
Standing.

Then went back
To thinking about
More important things.

Flying off, the birds
Had already
Moved on.

Forgotten, yet still
Embraced,
I turned

A part of me left forever in the wood.

Reclaiming the Witch

What is a witch? Who?
Woman, wif: female person
Who's wildness? Lost, yet untamed
Wisdom, held
Within.

Intuitive intelligence; an
Inner strength, something
Intangible, immeasurable, yet
Intrinsically powerful:
'I'.

Transformative,
Transcending
The no-more-than-assistant role wer-man once
cast for her: he sees
Trouble, perceived as threat
To testosterone-heavy ego...tables are turning

Changeable as the seasons, curious,
Constantly creative,
Connected connately to Earthly cycles,
Capable of immense compassion, or
Cruelty

Hear her now.
Hear her howl, fury released from the
Hobbles she's been bound by, the
Hurt of centuries
Healing, as she hereafter finds
Herself,
Here.

Teatime with Mother

(after 'The Old Vicarage, Grantchester' by
Rupert Brooke)

Stands the clock at ten to three,
And is there honey still for tea?

"Honey? Yes...but not a lot:
Your Aunt Matilda spilled the pot;
I think that you can have some jam -
Or did that go to Uncle Sam?
What's in this cupboard?…Marmite? No…
That looks like we're running low…
I did intend to bake a cake
- but, what with Freddie running late,
And Susannah's swimming classes,
(And not being able to find my glasses!)
This morning seemed to whizz right by;
And I had to shop with half an eye
On Thomas (cos he's At That Age)…
Which reminds me - where'd I put that sage
For Julia? I must remember that,
Let's make a note now…MIND THE CAT!!
The silly thing WILL sleep just there
Right in the way! Right. What a pair!
Now. What was it you want again?
I'm listening (where IS that pen…?)

Oh, honey! Yes, that's right…well, dear -
Let's put the kettle on. I fear
That all I have is toast
And butter (- spread -), or cheese, at most,
But that's quite nice, I think; and so
Is sitting down for just a mo,
With a cup of something - yes, let's sit
And have a rest for just a bit…
A cup of tea…Ahh that's the stuff!
You've got your toast? Is that enough?
So: what's the time now? Five to three…
Twenty minutes then…let's see,
Before I need to…hello Puss!
I knew you'd come to have a fuss
Made! Yes you're right, of course, I need
To Just Be A Lap - and breathe,
And take a minute not to 'Do'
- or Plan, or Worry…..gosh but Ju!
I wonder how she's doing? Oh!
Such a tricky time! I know,
I know; I must learn to let it go.
It's hard. Now how's your toast, dear? Good?
I'm sorry 'bout the honey, love. Would
You like some more? No? Happy? Lovely.
Look - this silly cat has gone all cuddly…
So, then, how are you?
You're very quiet there you know…?…"

Stands the clock at ten past three:

There's not much honey - but there's tea,
Belonging, warmth, love, spread and toast
And the people that we need the most,
So may we find a little time
To sit and 'be' for one short rhyme.
A moment, where we all unwind
Together and - perhaps - we'll find
A little peace, a memory,
A space to breath, some poetry…

The Farmers

They cleared the trees,
They ploughed the earth,
They sowed the corn,
A People's birth.

They saw the land,
They took the stone,
They used their hands
And made it all their own.

In rings of Blue
And Sarsen tall:
The sun bathes gold
Ancestral hall.

Departing souls,
They honour then
In earth; in fire,
Now heavensent.

They saw the land,
They took their tools,
Each trodden step
Another fuels…

They saw the land
They took the stone,
They used their hands
And made it all their own.

They see the land;
These Sarsens great,
Remind us that
The earth's our fate.

The Holly and The Ivy:
Retold

(after 'The Holly and the Ivy' traditional
Christmas carol)

The holly and the ivy,
When they are both full grown,
Of all the trees in the greenwood
The holly bears the crown.

Oh the holly bears a blossom,
As white as falling snow,
Now tell again the story
Of a child born long ago.

Oh the holly bears a berry
As blood-red as a wound,
So gather close together,
For darkness falls too soon.

Oh the holly bears a prickle
As sharp as any knife,
And green leaves through midwinter,
To tell of new year's life.

Oh the holly bears a wood
That burns so warm and bright,

So gather close and sing out loud
Against the winters night!

Gardnery Ellen

(after 'Barbara Ellen' traditional English ballad)

'Twas early, early all in the Spring,
The green buds all were growing,
So I went down to the Hardware Store,
For to get some seeds for sowing.

I sowed my seeds, and I sowed them well,
And very soon they were growing,
But then I found I had better be
Quickly getting hoe-ing.

Oh I love my garden, I love it well.
It gives me so much pleasure,
And I will always happy be -
If daisies be the measure.

I hoe'd them weeds, aye, I hoe'd them well,
I thought them I was quelling,
I hoe'd so much that my hands turned green,
And they called me 'Gardnery Ellen'.

I hoe'd them weeds, aye, I hoe'd them well,
Because my seeds they was smothering
While the sun shone warm, and the rains fell
soft,

Oh I saw those bee-flies a-hovering.

Aye the sun shone warm; but the rains fell
wetter,
And the weeds grew strong and lusty,
But my little plants didn't fare so well
- in fact they turned quite rusty...

"Oh! You are sick! And you're very sick -
Dear plant, I fear you're dying!
I should have gone to 'Dobies',
And better seed been buying."

Then the rains did stop! But the sun shone
brighter -
I thought my plants were frying;
My face burned red, and my arms did too,
And greatly I was sighing.

And the weeds still grew, they grew high, and
higher,
All day I'd spend a-hoeing;
And I hoe'd so well, but my back did ache
 - and the lawn still needed mowing...

And the weeds STILL grew! They grew high;
and higher -
All day I spent a-weeding,
I wish I'd picked an indoor hobby,

For to go outside I was dreading.

Oh I love my garden, I love it well,
Though it gives me little pleasure,
Yet I would always happy be,
If daisies were the measure...

And my plants grew sick, Oh! So very sick,
I heard the death-bells knelling,
And I knew they'd never better be,
Though my name be 'Gardnery Ellen'.

"Oh you are sick, aye, you're very sick,
Dear plants! I think you're dying,
And you will never better be
- but it's not for my want of trying!

"Oh Mother, Mother! Make my bed,
I fear the battle's ending…
The squirrels launched a surprise attack
And I see the crows descending!"

My Mother made me a lovely bed
So cosy that I fell in,
When I wake again I will change my name,
No, I'll never be Gardnery Ellen.

But I love my garden, aye, I love it well,
And still it gives me pleasure,

And I will always happy be,
For daisies are my measure.

October Garden

The last of the nasturtiums
Reflect October's pale sun,
As it peers over the pine trees
On the hill. Bright bursts of flame,
In the vegetable bed;
Little glimmers of a
Welcome warmth
Before winter sets in.

Safe The Ewes

The sky it is blue and the sun it shines gold,
Oh light the fire my dear,
Down fall the leaves, for the summer is old,
Now safe the ewes' grazing.

Yellow and green turn russet and red,
Oh, light the fire my dear,
The Winter King's waking out of his bed,
Now keep safe the ewes' grazing

The corn is brought in and stored in the barn,
Oh light the fire my dear,
And the hay is all mown, stacked up safe from
harm,
And, safe, the ewes' grazing.

Green still the grass, and fat grown my lambs,
Oh, light the fire my dear,
And steady, bright-eyed, waiting, my rams
Oh safe the ewes' grazing.

For the wheel it rolls on, and day becomes night
Now light the fire my dear,
But so night becomes day - and the fire burns
bright,

Keep safe the ewes' grazing.

Down in green pasture, under the trees,
Oh, light the fire my dear,
Sheltered from storms and from the cold autumn
breeze,
There - safe, my ewes', grazing.

Shipyard

Yesterday down by the river:
Men building great ships to cross the sea
Yesterday, down by the river:
A great harbour for a great industry.

But the tide keeps rolling on,
And time just keeps rolling by,
The river meets the sea,
Where the ships sail
Away from me.

Today as you stroll by the river,
The craftsman's cry is no longer heard,
The skilled men have gone; the yard stands
silent
The only sound the cry of a bird.

Dream

25

Dream, organic being.

I have left the darkness on transparent lines.
More sense wanting integrity, yes, birth
simplicity.
Solution - this the beautiful delicacy
Beyond his horizons.
Recognise weakness without taking force:
The lifetime takes complicated flexibilities.

During a Scottish Winter

Water
Rushing,
Shifting,
Chopping,
Never stopping,
Constantly cogitating
Silver
Against the dim,
Muted,
Monochromatic
January grey. A robin
Breathes out song
One murmur of colour
- gone.
Under my feet,
A blade of grass
Carefully
Balancing
It's procession of
Perfect
Shining
Baubles:
These fragile globes
Rain
Temporarily transfixed,
Momentarily
At rest.

Sunbeam

A sunbeam
Dances through the canopy
Above, green leaves glowing

Golden, light passes
Warming the dark earth
Beneath, for a moment's knowing.

Mote by dusty, shimmering mote,
It doesn't seem much
But

It is enough
To change my mind.

Trust

Who?
How?
To tell which are those
Who have no shadows? Those
Who appear as men under the
Broad light of day; but
Under the pale gleam of the moon
Dissolve
Into shadowless spectres,
As delusive as the heroes they dissemble.
When the bright sun dims
And Night
 - With all her terrors -
Darkly falls,
Who, then,
Will remain solidly
Beside me,
Ready heart beating,
Silvery stubborn shadow
At their feet
Faithful as a wolfhound;
A guard against predators unseen
As yet, until
Time
Shifts again and

Night
Becomes Day...
Until the moon shines
How will I tell?
Who has no shadow?

Midwinter

Marking the deep, dark centre of the year
In hushed moments amidst the festive cheer,
Drawing in, cosying up,
Warming toes, fingers and spirit before a
flickering flame,
I pause; and look up to the twinkling stars to
guide me through the coming
New Year. "Keep my footsteps safe and true
'midst all the next
Twelve months might bring".
Earth turns, and we must turn with her, through
summer full and winter thin.
Reflect, relax, re-gather and renew.

A Christmas Blessing

See the candle flicker,
Watch the bright flame burn.
It's cold and dark outside the door,
Yet we are safe and warm.

I thank you for this plate of food,
I thank you for my friends,
I thank you for my family,
The support and warmth they lend.

I thank you for these gifts received
For the love that I've been shown,
I thank you for the love I give,
That warmth is mine to own.

For darkness falls,
Yet, embers glow -
So let the light shine through
And, as we watch this candle flame,
May Christmas Blessings be with you.

www.ingramcontent.com/pod-product-compliance
Lightning Source LLC
Chambersburg PA
CBHW071239140726
47996CB00007B/2671